T0129008

Other books by the same author

Fiction

Novels
Conflict in the Home
Sauce of Life
Struggle Toward Extinction
Motivating Forces

Poetry
Poems (Flowery Country/Sun and Rain/Grains of Sand)

Non-Fiction

Memoir
Dark Days

Philosophy
Intrinsic to Universe
The Material Structure

Sayings
Reduced Reflections

Linguistics
LUIF: A New Language
LUIF Dictionaries

DIVERSE MODES

Poems by

Tan Kheng Yeang

Printed in the United States of America.

ISBN: 978-1-4669-1080-5 (sc)
ISBN: 978-1-4669-1081-2 (hc)
ISBN: 978-1-4669-1082-9 (e)

Library of Congress Control Number: 2012900003

Trafford rev. 04/20/2012

 www.trafford.com

North America & international
toll-free: 1 888 232 4444 (USA & Canada)
phone: 250 383 6864 ♦ fax: 812 355 4082

Contents

DIVISION ONE 1

    The Tiger 3

    Television 4

    The Kidnapping 6

    Fireman's Escapade 8

    Advice 10

    Nothing but Trouble 11

    Clothing 12

    Bank Robbery 13

    To the Mynah 15

    Swift and Sudden Death 16

    Ode to Lightning 17

    Angry Incident 19

    Shame 21

    Malice 23

    Kindness 24

    Hate 25

    Obstinacy 26

    The Optimist 27

    Love-Wrecked 28

    Obedience 29

    The Last Straw of Despair 30

    Anxiety 31

    Pity 32

    Fear 33

    Envy 34

DIVISION TWO 35

    Mess of a World 37

    Traffic Accident 38

    The Cheat 39

    The Mechanic 41

    The Money-Changer 42

    The Thief 43

    Stock Market 44

Flame of the Forest 46
The Rebel.. 47
Coast Road... 49
Tamarind 50
Rambutan... 51
Airport 52
Sauntering at Midnight... 54
Virtus Post Nummos... 56
Queues 58
Noise Everywhere 59
Symbol... 60
To Dream and Fail 61
Utility... 62
The State.. 63
Mentally Conquered 64
Welfare of the People... 66
Originality.. 67
News 69
Illusion... 70
The Wind 71
Waiting for Train... 72
Never Such Danger... 73
Ruins... 74

DIVISION THREE..**75**
Routine 77
Motorcycle... 78
Brickwork 79
Foundations.. 80
Traffic Signs 81
Environmental Pollution... 83
The Arch... 84
The Culvert... 85
Air... 86
Water... 87
Steam 89
Ice 90
Electricity 91
Sound.. 92
Retaining Wall 93
Hydrogen 94

Iron 95
Magnet 97
Paint 99
Glass 101
Granite 103
Concrete 104
Aluminium 106
Asphalt 107
Light 108
Carbon 110
Clouds 111
Lithosphere 112
Heat 113
Nitrogen 115
Sodium 116
Trigonometry 118
Weathering 119
Copper 121
Chlorine 123
Rocks 124
Fossils 126
Photosynthesis 128
Energy 130
Clay 131
Limestone 133
Asbestos 135

DIVISION FOUR **137**
Circling of Island 139
The Tragedy of Life 143
The Parking Attendant 146

Acknowledgement

"The author wishes to thank Ms. Valerie Cameron for her invaluable assistance in preparing the manuscript of this book for publication."

Diverse Modes

Diverse Modes, a four-part anthology of verse, truly lives up to its name, presenting an array of poetic styles and themes.

Divisions One and Two are written in ordinary free verse, while Divisions Three and Four explore two unique and highly innovative forms developed by the author: verse in which sentences have no finite verbs and "amorphous verse", which is the same as prose in style, but retains the lyricism of poetry in terms of language.

The author's keen sense of observation takes the reader on a fascinating journey—from the glories and the terrors of nature to the wide range of human emotions and experience to the unique qualities of so-called mundane objects that most of us fail to notice in the rush of everyday life.

His insight extends to the fundamental components of life and the universe. Using words as simple building blocks, as strong and elemental as the subjects themselves, he creates not only a powerful image of their physical qualities but captures and fixes their distinct essence in the mind of the reader.

Division One

The Tiger

The farmer outside his hut stands begrimed,
A dark expanse of jungle behind;
Firewood splits log by weary log
Following the rhythmic motion of his axe;
Hot sweat vociferates from his strenuous frame,
And his muscles are tense with strain.

A tiger stands on a bush-covered knoll
Distant scarce twenty yards to the right,
Motionless, slowly rolling its fell
Visage towards the surroundings, then on the man
Directing a concentrated gaze of strength.

Instinctively the man turns round,
Sees the flaming hide streaked with night;
Immobility locks his limbs;
When his disrupted senses resume their note,
A fearful scream bursts through his floodgate.

Tiger leaps with agile force,
Man wild with dread attempts to run;
It apprehends his head with its paws,
Mauls savagely and strikes him dead;
In pieces the human being disappears,
Massively the beast slinks back into the jungle.

Television

Achievements throng the hall of science,
None more splendid than television shines;
That scenes could be transmitted through wide space,
Had it not actually occurred,
Would be incredible even to the wise.

What purpose has this triumph served—
Marvellous good, notable work?
Wondrous advertisements splash across the screen—
Strangely nutritious this brand of milk,
Those biscuits are unique,
This car travels with the smoothest speed;
That bicycle is extremely cute;
This detergent makes the dirtiest clothing white,
That paint is the most durable ever made,
Such coolness emerges from no other fan,
Summit efficiency dwells in the fridge on view.

Listen to the politicians as they prate,
Limping with inanity and platitude;
They talk of what they don't understand—
Ideas and ideals for the good of man;
They understand what they don't talk—
The way to get a share of the cake.

Forums and discussions by panels
Of dull so-called experts
From whom fair words distil—
Obvious ideas and trite observations;
Come quizzes of diverse kinds,
Showing you live inside or outside your mind,
Or whether as spouse you deserve reward or fine.

The delight of millions of fans,
Stories forming regular series.
Cowboys of the past century
Staunchly tending cows? No!
Fighting waved their real bent.
Detectives of colossal acumen
Doughtily solving crimes in triumph,
Dexterous with their fists,
Exempt from death though overcome.
Dreary sketches that don't seem funny,
Still every sentence induces laughter's chime.

TV as an invention is hard to beat
And its results—what better can one get!

The Kidnapping

He breathes the leader of a tiny band,
His temper intractable and violent;
A school dropout he much preferred the life
Of a street urchin—wily tricks,
Fisticuffs, pilfery formed his days;
He gravitated into the dens of crime.

Meticulous inquiries are set afloat
Before a person is selected for prey;
Maleficent work no less than good eats time;
Shouldn't the victim feel honoured to be
The subject of such anxious interest?
He doesn't know the existence of his host.

Time is at hand and he fleetly strikes;
As the hapless man steps into his car,
Tickles a pistol on his nape
And grates a voice behind his ear;
Enter two more emerging from elsewhere.

His eyes are bandaged, the car is driven out
To a deserted road some miles from town;
It rolls to an unpretentious attap hut,
Curtly the man is shoved into a room
And locked in to enjoy his thoughts alone.

Tan Kheng Yeang

His captors are to him but sound,
Sometimes his guard appears with mask on face;
Limbs motionless, a tight gag in his mouth,
Terror alternates with dreariness;
Despair remorselessly grows as the hours pass;
Why they have taken him is a mystery,
Whether he is scheduled for death—who knows?

Phone rings and the victim's father hears
In a few dreadful words of his son's plight;
Failing delivery of the sum demanded—
Cash in a bag to be duly brought
To a specific place by the time set—
Family will not see their own again.

Warned not to notify the police
And caring for naught except the safe return,
Warily the father raises the currency
And has it sent as instructed on the phone.
Dusk and the victim is rapidly driven
To a secluded spot within the town;
Dazed he stands alone on the roadside
As he removes the bandage when
He hears the sound of the retreating car;
Dully he makes his way home, where he lies
Like a stricken animal in its lair.

Fireman's Escapade

Six years a fireman, a captive to his work,
Enjoyable, thrilling, most exciting;
He loves to see the flames that greedily bake
Inert, resistless buildings roaring triumph,
Unmercifully grinding down their prey;
He loves to bring them to extinguishment;
Busily moving round, he spins his tasks
Gleefully—holding a hose and spouting water,
Climbing tall ladders, rushing into ruins—
With the crowd gaping in the background he
Feels great; he is not short on vanity.

For long succession of days no fires have burst
And drilling at his station is all his work—
Tiresome, senseless, a frightful fardel.
Terrible to think! No smokers now exist
To fling away nonchalant cigarette butts?
Are all electric circuits free of faults?
Are there no arsonists to generate welts
Of burning mischief? All men have become
Good, careful, rational—or so things seem.

He feels immensely restless—this will not do;
A reckless thought suddenly spans his face;
A little distance from his station lies
A recently vacated bungalow;
Dark night—shortly before he goes on
Duty he cycles to the grassy site
Carrying a small can of kerosene;
Carefully, pouring it behind the house,
The wooden doors and windows he sets alight;
Swiftly he cycles to his station to wait.

Slowly the hapless building starts to burn,
Fire spreads, some time elapses ere a neighbour
Finds it and promptly rings the station;
The swift fire engine clangours to the scene;
The red flame climbing higher and higher roars,
The hoses spout cold water without stint,
The crowd that has assembled from nowhere stares,
The incendiary is in his element,
Joy dances in his heart at the irony:
He made the fire, and he is smothering it.

Advice

Advice is easy to diffuse,
As its effect does not redound
On the giver; nil is its cost,
While it confers an aura
Of wisdom at its best;
A ready and popular pastime
For fool and sage alike.

Scarcely ever original in idea,
Such as has probably swept
The victim's mind before,
Its efficacy is doubtful.

Not taking into account the advice,
Which is subtly peeled from malice,
Even the sincerest form
Must not be accepted without thought,
For it must needs be born
Of the giver's limited, possibly slight,
Knowledge and experience
And ineradicable prejudice.

Advice sits on the same
Abject platform as criticism,
Seldom of any value,
Generally made by the vacuous,
Rarely dropping nutritious fruit
For the recipient.

Best to refrain from imparting it,
Save in response to earnest request,
And then only after tilling
Assiduously the soil of cogitation,
The sole concern
The welfare of the other person.

Nothing but Trouble

Life is nothing but trouble:
Let one grow an ambition,
And to bring it to fruit
He wears his heart out,
Endures toil and privation,
Only to fall to the hammer of despair.

Life is one long trouble:
The body, like a machine,
Links a multiplicity of parts;
Let but one organ go astray
And what accrues is pain.

Life is endless trouble:
Prosperity bathes a man
And he is basking in the noon
Of joy when a seeming trifle
Churns into a calamity,
Chance determining his lot.

Life is trouble fold on fold:
Some are caused by nature,
Which is far from mild;
Most are of man's own nurture
From folly and malevolence;
It may be great or small,
But never stops its wretched tunes.

Clothing

Every country in every age displays
Its peculiar style of dress.
Down through the centuries
Struts the amazing variety;
Such ingenuity and imagination
Must needs evoke condemnatory praise.

The beauty of apparel, its charm
Tinkles only to the illusory eye.
The trimmings and decorations that aim
To captivate are unnatural.

Clothing protects from cold
But does not lessen heat.
Constant use has made it stand
As a synonym for decency.
A beneficial article has become
Vanity's fascinating theme.

Bank Robbery

The bank announces its edifice
In a long straight asphalted street
Where traffic oscillates to and fro;
In the vicinity to the right
Numerous ships and diverse restaurants
Narrate a tale of buoyant business.

The afternoon sun shows bright and hot,
And the bank is nearing time to close
Its doors to customers when a cigarette
Fast in his mouth and a green case
Dangling blithely from his hand,
A youth comes stepping in apace—
Dandified, slight of build,
Displaying a genial countenance.

He casts a cursory look around
And, walking up to a counter, brings
Haltingly out a folded cheque
As though to present it for cashing;
Then fleetly a pistol flashes forth,
Levelled at the cashier's mouth.

Simultaneously three men,
Singly having entered earlier
And stationed themselves at diverse spots,
Assert their prowess with knife and pistol;
One deftly disarms the stolid guard
Who is sustaining a clumsy gun,
And one glowers, a thorough cad
Holding the manager at his desk.

The hapless boss instructs his men
To slide all the recalcitrant cash with them
Into the greedy case
Inflicted by the robber chief.
A paralysing robe of stark
Terror has muffled staff and clients alike.

The miscreants make for the door
And hasten into the street;
No stiff policeman wanders near,
And scurrying passersby know not
Of what explodes within their sight.

The joy-swept desperadoes speedily climb
Onto a couple of motorcycles
Waiting efficiently near the building's rim,
Engrave with screeches a calm side street
Fewer than ten fleet yards away
From the original moneyed scene,
And noisomely fade out of the town.

To the Mynah

Guest of the garden, you love
To walk and stroll around
Gallantly on two noiseless feet;
With bobbing head raised in proud front
Gaily and briskly you survey the scene.

Your colouring is a distinctive charm,
Your plumage has dark brown for theme,
White tips your tail and on either
Wing interpolates a patch;
Below your eyes gold shows its gleam.

Now you suddenly fly
To that low cassia tree
With beautiful yellow flowers;
Now you descend to walk and run;
Off lightly you fly again
Onto the hibiscus hedge.

Gem of content and peace,
You find all things so sweet—
Sun, breeze, flowers, grass;
What is your silent secret?
Perforce I must believe your mind
Plays only with enamouring thoughts.

Blitheness without surcease of yours
Brighter than the noonday sun
Engenders responsive joy in me;
When I see you, my care
Vanishes like momentary foam;
I lose my weariness and gloom.

Swift and Sudden Death

In a goldsmith's shop a rancorous robber
Was holding him stupefied with a pistol;
He was to disencumber his till
And scoop up the jewellery nearest him.

Tremblingly, panic-struck, the man
Delivered in a paper bag;
Towards the entrance the villain backed
Threateningly with eyes ablaze.

A detective chancing to be in the place
Rushed out a pistol in hot haste,
Purpose to threaten the miscreant,
Who swiftly turned and, firing first,
Slew him and instantly disappeared.

Ode to Lightning

Oh, glittering marvel of the sky!
You burst in momentary flash,
Never prolonging your feral stay;
I thrill to your presence, your mesh
Of fetterless exuberant joy,
Your strange display of sublimity.

More than mere electricity,
Might in majestic form are you,
Made visible, grown wild,
You traveller from cloud to cloud
Or cloud to ground.

What may you be in actual truth,
Mystery of mysteries?
Your unrelenting magnificent strength
Moves me with apprehensive wonder;
You rank not just a natural force
But the riddle of the universe.

Thunder, your raucous fraternal twin,
Hammers the ear to panicky fright,
But he just sports a harmless whim
Unlike you, fleet of foot,
Danger to tree and man,
Dissevered terror roaming space.

The earth is shot with passion and tense
When you perform your spasmodic dance;
Jarred by your onslaught, the frail sky
Jerks open to let you rush your way.

Nothing can beat the vertiginous
Nomadic rapture you feel and give
As you brandish your zigzag path
And thrust your bifurcations forth;
You rock and terrify my mind,
Impressing it with joy like pain.

What signifies your skyey ballet?
That force is Nature's goading essence,
Unrest is life's orbit's sun,
The life of matter and of man.

Angry Incident

He published an irascible man;
He hacked out insult from a word
And scented a sneer in a silent grin;
He was interminably alert
For subtle kicks at his defeats;
Failing to catch an utterance clearly,
He somersaulted the words for worst.

One day while jarring a seat in a park
With his habitual toothache look,
A stranger suddenly appeared
And heavily sat down beside
While munching jackfruit fritters from
A plastic bag crammed to the brim.

On finishing his oily meal
He tossed away the frolicsome bag
Which kissed by a light gentle breeze
Went dancing wildly in full sail
The other person's face to blot.

With truculent anger round turned the man
Raucously barking, "You think you could
Recklessly fling at people filth?"
The stranger: "Sorry! I didn't mean
To throw it at you. The wretched wind
Blew it astray." "Haven't you eyes
In your head? Could you not have cast
It on the ground beside your seat
If you are too slothful to walk
To refuse bin behind your back?"

"I truly blame myself, I was
Entirely in the wrong, excuse me."
"Regret makes not the less remiss
Your reprehensible laxity;
I think you could have had more sense
Than to make a dirty paper dance."

Continuing thus to speak, the more
Abuse he flung the angrier
He swelled; gesticulating wildly
His odd behaviour was as though
Hysteria galloped in his brain.
Mute, open-mouthed, the stranger gazed
In consternation and surprise;
Never had he met one like this;
He rose and hastily moved away.

The peppery man unloosed one last
Volley of fast vituperation,
Then mutteringly sauntered off
Right in the opposite direction;
Heedless of his disgruntled steps
He stumbled over a puddle,
Hit his round head against a tree
Hard by and dropped, a lifeless frame.

Shame

Shame twisted into a skein his days,
His crooked teeth sliced into his brain,
His receding chin was shaped to harass,
His lack of wealth was paramount shame,
His weak physique made strong regret,
His family spelled pure embarrassment.

Hurriedly pushing his steps along
He jolted an acquaintance in the street,
Whose wall of face constructed of sneers
Betokened a malicious spirit;
Abruptly he paused when the other did.

"Where could you be proceeding
With such unseemly haste?"
Thus the quizzical acquaintance.
"Is there a bag of gold
Flashing at end of road?
Or maybe a beautiful girl
Submerged in sea of love?"

"Hurry is stranger to my intent,
My destination is only the bank."
"I see. You are going to make a great
Deposit. Why not be generous
And stand me a little treat?"
"Dearth separates me from such a move."
"Poverty grips you in its claws,
No doubt revolves round it, I suppose."

The man was slashed by blushing shame,
He felt his poverty magnetized fun,
He heard his clothing's shabby chime,
Comparing it with the other's terylene
Trousers and polyester shirt
Of recent fashionable out.

Suddenly all the ills of his life
Coagulated into a baneful brick
Heavily pressing down his mind;
Clearing without further ado
From the agonizing site,
Almost running he sped straight
To a sequestered corner
Taut with strain of the coastal road;
He leaped into the sea,
Drowning his voluminous shame.

Malice

Malice in him evolved to a rare degree,
Its exercise was pleasure's cream;
People he scanned for their defects
And gloatingly to view hauled them;
He never fluttered a pennant of praise,
When stroked by him gold turned to dross.

Went he forth to a club meeting
With no desire for common good,
Aim the officials to distress
And all their actions to criticize,
To make their motives seem devious;
Numerous questions sailed in reckless stream,
Noise spread its wings around the hall.

He queried the accounts
Of fraud dispersing hints;
Flashing with anger the treasurer
Frostily asked him what he meant;
The reply, his meaning was quite plain,
Especially to the affected man.

The treasurer forward sturdily stepped
And ere one fathomed his intent,
With a sharp blow he knocked him down;
Commotion the assembly gripped;
Some blamed the treasurer while most
Scoffed at the malicious pest
Who dared not strike back in return
But rose and almost ran,
His heart a fardel of chagrin.

Kindness

He thought: "We live but a brief time,
Life is a crushing flame,
Why snare a person in misery's net?
When one can turn aside a blade
Slicing a fellow man, it should be done,
Kindness is the iodine
Healing life's wounds."

Walking along a cliff, he noted
Wearing a tribulation look
A figure sitting near the brim—
He was acquainted with his ill name—
Rancorous, unscrupulous,
Recently chained to insolvency,
Who had once defrauded him;
He had disliked him since.

Perfunctory glance and he
Did not slacken in his walk;
Then curious he turned to look;
Pierced with fright he saw the man
Preparing to leap into the sea.

Back with alacrity he sprang
And round his body firmly flung
His arms. "What's on your mind?"
The speechless other slumped to the ground
And rested his forehead on his hand.

He garnered a tale of futile struggle,
Of privation and misery;
Hope he injected with kindly sense,
Offering monetary aid;
He welcomed him to his abode
To stay until he could make good.

Hate

His heart is caged in hate,
Never has anybody lit his night,
Humanity is one vile mass,
Happiness is not his lot;
An orphan reluctantly reared
By a harsh uncle, a cad,
He bolted from his home.

A clerk in an insurance firm,
He sifts no pleasure from his work,
He wishes to be free, not to conform
To rancid routine, strongly to seek
Adventure, but he vainly frets,
Anarchy in his heart and brain.

Dissatisfied with him, his boss
Delivers a lecture full of spite;
His hatred blows a hurricane,
With furious hand he knocks him down—
What matters his job with paltry pay?
A wanderer he will be.

Obstinacy

Persistence in what is wrong is his,
Plastic behaviour is against his grain,
Into an argument should he slide
He must strut out with the last word;
If an erroneous course of action
Inveigles him, he must inhabit it;
His watchword is "No change."

Disputing with a close friend
About a political problem,
Which hooks their interests but little,
He gets emotional, violent,
Hotly exudes insults.

Returning home he irefully
Recounts the incident to his wife;
She explains in patient tone
And makes his thought incline
That wrong he might have done;
But his crass obstinacy
Demands resistance to apology;
He earns a permanent enemy.

The Optimist

Optimism is a major producer
Of happiness the while it rings,
But with adamantine knocks,
Interminable kicks,
Its tone sounds ludicrous.

Born an inflexible optimist,
If he loses at the casino,
Belief infiltrates him; his luck
Next time will blossom anew;
His car collides with another,
Hurt but with life intact,
Such accident he thinks
Surely won't leap again.

His wife abandons him
And tramps off with another man,
Convinced he is she will return,
She won't put him to shame,
But giving her her due
She is just on a holiday.

He deems all troubles he will survive
And his will be a lengthy life;
Germs, accidents, calamities,
Natural or man-made,
Jar him they may but not annul,
Plane crash and death are at his side.

Love-Wrecked

They meet and fall in love,
Two strangers from different towns;
What makes them to each other cleave?
Turbulent mystery, who can unravel?

She is betrothed to a man of wealth
Of whom her parents strongly approve,
He is divided from a wife
Obdurate in refusing to divorce him;
He tells his tale to her, she hers,
No murky concealment is.

They stroll around for half a year
Before her fiancé stumbles on the truth;
Treading the injured path
He cuts the slack string causing her
Parents to grumble and glare.

Dragging on their compulsive affair,
Devoid of any sunny solution,
They slide from relatives and friends
Who look at them askance;
Willfully he neglects his work,
Woeful loss of job ensues;
With hands together locked
Into the sea they jump love-wrecked.

Obedience

He tractable obedience addict rates,
He wags tail where authority resides,
Doctrine just sculptured for the power-mad;
Obedience in itself is not a virtue,
Obedience to the evil is pure evil,
Desolate slavery of the thoughtless mind.

With a dark terrorist band he makes his home,
His will no longer flutters as his own,
He captive to his leader sits
Whose orders readily he effectuates;
Most abject of ridiculous underlings
Mysteriously he fancies he is great,
Mighty compared to those outside the pale.

His leader charges him to execute
A stranger he has never met
But said to be a peril to the group,
Though truly just a personal enemy.
Briskly he grips the errand, kicking questions off;
Thus he displays his dutiful principle.

Diligently he ferrets facts about his victim,
At night he stealthily tracks him to his home;
Prowling around the large sequestered compound,
Planning the accurate time to shoot,
Suddenly leaps on him a surly dog,
Scaring him mauled and wounded away.

Impatient with what he deems incompetence,
His leader wrathfully sends him from the band;
Imminent apprehension by police
And thinking force might make him leak his mind,
Impassively he has him fleetly killed;
A genuine virtue thrives on reciprocity;
Obedience tends to burst the dam of tyranny.

The Last Straw of Despair

Despair enmeshes his every part
And rolls him in its dirt;
His business slides to a pit of bankruptcy,
Horrible miseries blow relentlessly;
Cancer is gobbling up his wife;
Crushing his son is drug addiction.

Every dog is said to have its day,
But not this specimen;
Of life's gifts he has never had his due,
Born loser is what he has always been.

Instinctive is the love of life;
He struggles sturdily on in grief
Without a hope of better days,
Worn out he still must wrestle with his fate
For his wife's sake
And welfare of his children.

A car comes roaring down the street
And kills his little daughter, aged eight;
Suddenly hearing the terrible news,
Stricken he gives a piercing cry;
Sanity flees from his demolished mind.

Anxiety

Anxiety ties a knot in his heart
And moans a dirge in his slow feet,
No pleasure he tastes in anything,
Nags sister worry day and night.

He has procured a bundle of shares
On a rosy tip from a friend,
The waves of a boom are lapping the shores
Of the euphoric tireless market,
And this particular company
Hums louder prosperity.

He has succeeded in wheedling a loan
From a reluctant bank to gain
Ownership of the counter;
Odious thought! But should mischance befall
Sundered from him would be his fortune.

He reads the financial news with greed,
Listens rapt to the radio
And spends religiously his time inside
Lively stockbrokers' offices
Just knowledge of dubious worth to glean
About the economic situation,
The share market's dizzy tide
And the particular aid
To wealth he has acquired.

His runaway anxiety
Is not his to defy,
He babbles of his hopes and fears,
Hunting for sympathy;
Finally a nervous breakdown
Flagellates him for his folly.

Pity

Pity is said to be veiled contempt;
Paucity of disdain makes it
Just invisible,
Genuine pity knows no airs,
What grasps contempt is merely
Wearing ignobly pity's badge.

For others' sorrow comes to him,
From his abundant kindliness
He feels pity and sympathy,
Not flowing from superiority,
The cause is common humanity;
Foretell who can he may be in their state.

Walking along a country road
He hears cries from an attap hut,
Lured near he sees a man and woman
Lying dead with gunshot wounds and
Loudly crying two small children.

Pity sets free its current in his heart,
And tears bedew his countenance wet,
He makes report to the police,
Who find the case as one of murder,
Person and cause unknown;
He takes the children home
To rear them as his own.

Fear

Fear isn't a noble emotion,
Free though from it none is;
The power to press it under control,
That is what properly matters;
Helplessly giving way to its wild sweep
Is folly of destructive shape.

Bravery is not his—
Battered with fear of nightmares,
Afraid of harsh opprobrium,
Wary of hornets stinging him,
Oppressed by thoughts of pain,
Horrified at the prospect of death;
His fears are numerous and strong,
In him cymbals of misery clang.

His greatest, most persistent dread
Is sudden, violent death;
Fearful of claws and teeth he never
Follows a trail into a jungle;
Crashing planes are unbelievably grim
And so he never flies in them;
Visions arise of tumbling down if he
Ventures to walk along a cliff;
He shivers and turns pale
Just thinking a robber might choose to call.

Always a careful man,
He is walking along a pavement when
A motorcycle comes with frightening speed,
Swerves madly and rushes straight at him,
And over him rolls its restless load;
Sudden fear hits him and he dies.

Envy

Envy is a silly trait
That only serves to sting the harbourer,
Making his life a blight;
Worthless it is but all too common,
Its fruits are evil and misery;
Ill-naturedly it sunders man from man.

Flooded with envy he is of him,
Favoured with greater wealth than he,
Forlorn he doesn't set out to earn more;
His heart is filled with hate for him
Who is more knowledgeable, but
He doesn't care to learn;
With spite his mind revolves
When he sees one whom people praise;
What does he do to net the same? Nil.

Miserably he has a colleague who
Meandered into his firm at a later time
But got promoted over his head;
His envy swells and all that's bad
He wishes on him, but the reverse
Eventuates—or so it seems.

Comes the time when the colleague
Captures the post of chief;
In envy so completely sunk
His thoughts hover on murder's brink;
Held back by fear of consequences
He frets and fumes in secret.
A miserable life he lives,
And into death he raves.

Division Two

Mess of a World

What a mess of a world
To stroll in, gaze or cut apart!
Everywhere the human cars collide,
Wealth and power the consuming aspiration,
Wrangling, grappling, or annihilating.

Fellow creatures roll in mutual malignment
And bulge with envy at others' gain;
Robbers explode their violence,
Beggars plead their hungry cause on pavements,
Prostitutes trade their inexhaustible merchandise,
The unemployed vainly knock at locked gates,
The employed deliberately forge inactivity to steel demands.

War hurtles its flaming rockets,
If not in this raucous corner
Then in that unsuspected nook;
Small nations strut pugnacity
And gesticulate grandiose verbosity;
Superpowers prod their clients,
Vilify one another,
Manufacture munitions
And generously fly them into the conflict.

Can a turbulent globe
Girdled by ruthless economic motives,
Distorted by politicians and soldiers,
Leashed to the cult of power,
Dictators or demagogues,
Enjoy any genuine good? Genuine good?
Truly a mess of a world!

Traffic Accident

A car on a minor road
Hastening to reach its destination,
Perpetually in a hurry,
Arrives pantingly at a junction
And, scarcely deigning to pause for breath,
Palpitates onto the main road.

Another car exuberant on the main road
Hastening to reach its destination,
Perpetually in a hurry,
Bounces glowingly towards the junction
And confidently veers onto the other road.

A crash of negligence
And both cars stutter to a halt;
Wreckage of metal,
Splintering of glass,
Concussion, fractured limbs, bleeding bodies
For drivers and passengers—
What has become of the hurry?

The Cheat

He perambulates the pavement,
Sifting the swirling crowd around;
Reflection stings him—
If he doesn't consummate a coup
Within the few days rushing to appear
He will be near the pit of insolvency;
No bar, turf, or casino;
Indeed he may even have
To forfeit his meals.

His glum eyes measure the passersby,
Light tinkles music into them
As he scans a slow-moving man
With a cigarette in his mouth
Sauntering complacently toward him,
A man of moneyed look
And nude of subtlety—
A made-to-order victim.

A cigarette on tiptoe between his fingers,
He pins the nincompoop for a light;
As it stutters into glow
He releases the casual remark
The other is born to luck;
The victim surprised
Distils a look of interrogation;
The cheat smiles and asseverates,
His physiognomy megaphones his future.
He waves him into a coffee shop.

With drinks on table
The trickster unfolds a scheme of wealth—
To set in motion a factory
For the production of textiles.
He is shaping a company,
Five other persons have handed assent,
Persons of repute and substance whom he names.
The dupe gravitates into enrolment as a partner.

Preliminary expenses needs must hum—
Printing a diversity of documents,
Renting an office of presentable mien,
Hiring a clerk for a start;
The gull agrees to pay his share.

His home squats just a score houses away,
The swindler dances along with alacrity
And grips the joyous money;
They part with kindest expressions—
The victim searches for him in vain.

Tan Kheng Yeang

The Mechanic

The workshop is a plantation
Of living machines and lathes,
All talking away with raucous garrulity;
Here one man is turning a rod;
There another is drilling holes in a plate.

The day is afflicted with heat,
And rain has not even whispered for weeks;
The workshop, where no fans spin coolness,
Reeks with dismalness,
A sloven in a coat of oil and grime,
And the cacophony of machinery
Reveals sound in its obnoxious aspect.

This particular mechanic,
In physique lithe, in mind sprightly,
Is manipulating a machine
Whose specific job is tool-sharpening;
Zealously occupied the whole day,
He is now the prey of fatigue;
He scans the clock on the wall—
Almost time for departure.

An approaching colleague sharply calls his name,
Prodding him to whirl abruptly round;
His hand is trapped in the revolving mechanism,
A scream of agony the reaction;
He wrenches back his arm,
And the hand is no longer his,
Severed by the unfeeling monster.

41

The Money-Changer

Ensconced behind a counter he sits
Beside his case of foreign notes;
Here hurries a tourist
Who desires to change his Australian currency
For Malaysian legal tender.
That transaction terminates,
And here pops in a local man
Who wants American money,
Chaffers and departs.
What work does he perform
Genuinely beneficial to others?
His trade is in response to a requirement
Or he would not enjoy a niche
In the present social structure.
But what task does he accomplish
Of productive import?

The Thief

The sky will soon muffle
The scanty stars that chatter still;
The murky air is cool
Round the houses of all types and sizes
Where the folks lie senseless in sleep;
He walks along a skulking figure,
One dark thought churning in his mind.

It sits undistinguished—one of a row;
Why does he pick it as prey?
He has with assiduous scrutiny
Perambulated the neighbourhood
And comes to know this and that.
Prising open the rear door
He stands on the lucrative side of the wall.

Treading round in invisible silence
He lifts a transistor radio from a table
And a valuable fountain pen;
Silkily pushing a gap in a door
He peers into a bedroom,
Seizes a diamond ring,
Extracts a purse.

Emerging into the hall
And on his stealthy way out,
He swiftly uncloses the purse
And avidly peruses its contents;
The light of his torch
Publishes a smiling wad of notes.
Quickly along the asphalted unlighted lane
He propels his nefarious steps home.

Stock Market

The air-conditioned hall vociferates with chairs
Whose wooden popularity
With the overflowing crowd assembled there
Bespeaks the volume of trade;
People stand even in the passageway;
All have their gaze taken captive by the boards
With their rows of names and figures;
The stockbrokers behind their prosperous counters
Bawl into the restless telephones.

The bull market is climbing the Himalayas;
Prices have been exhaustlessly
Flying upwards for months—
Truly an exciting season;
A minor dip
And then a major jump—
Has the steep road a termination?
That is an academic question;
Consider only the present—
That seems to be the prevailing view.

The insensate scramble for shares
Is the game of the moment;
Buy—that is the abracadabra,
The open sesame to wealth;
Everyone charges into the fray
And prates glibly of the money he apprehends;
What a wondrous institution
Is the stock market!

It is strange, incredible,
The people who congregate there;
Besides the operators to whom
The exchange is a source of livelihood,
There are merchants whose business is teetering
On the verge of bankruptcy,
Hoping to capture a sufficiency

To ride a steady course again,
Professional men essaying to get rich,
Clerks disgusted with their congealed salaries,
Housewives who have lighted upon
A more gainful pastime than mah-jongg,
Pensioners trapped with excessive leisure.

At encounters, chance or otherwise,
In street or any other place,
The theme is the latest hot counter
Or new issue of unquestioned worth;
Dull companies performing uninspiring work
Are household words, magic names;
Folks lovingly reiterate
The mellifluous words, blue chips,
Which appear to be synonymous with bonanzas;
They are agog for tips,
Which are given and taken as certainties;
Bulls and stags are in their element.

Then the cataclysmic day
Like a tiger springs,
When without any premonition
The counters cascade in value
With portentous velocity;
Just a technical reaction,
Asseverate the wiseacres;
But the next day and the next
Selling, selling, and falling, falling;
The losses piercing the wall of disbelief
Ruthlessly zigzag their dizzy course downwards;
The bear market slithers along with a vengeance,
Hope of an upturn splutters out,
And despair twists tighter its grip
As one wretched day whines after another.

Flame of the Forest

Tall is this tree, ample, spreading,
With green feathery leaves,
Divided and again divided
Into tiny leaflets.

Open flat sprays of large flowers
Shine in all their scarlet beauty
And whisper enticing scent—
How gorgeous looks the tree
In its flaming array.

Standing under its shady boughs
This warm resolute evening,
Leaning against its smooth bark,
I feel the rush of stormy force
That makes it wildly sing
Its lovely blossomy triumph.

The Rebel

Born a rebel by nature
He execrates conformity;
Government is an imposture,
Society and its ways obnoxious;
To him a monotonous existence
Of routine, regular work,
Is the extreme of torture.

Dreaming of subverting the state
He finds oppressive,
He rushes into a secret society
Of rebels of similar intent—
His life is not felicity
But perilous, tremulous excitement.

He and his companions
Exhaust their time plotting,
Discussing this and that problem,
The strategy and tactics of revolt,
The way to ensnare power,
The strengthening of their party,
Propaganda among the masses.

Time smoothly rolls along,
Day after day flies,
Year after year runs.
He feels restless, morose;
His life seems wasted.
His erstwhile schoolmates
Are comfortably established
In their little niches,
While his achievement has been zero.

Still he will never relinquish
The seemingly fatuous strife;
Rebellion is in his blood,
No prosaic happiness for him,
Whatever the future may hold,
Success or failure,
Imprisonment or death—
He must struggle.

Coast Road

At the back of the sandy beach
Stands a row of casuarina trees,
Their tall frames spaced evenly apart
Parallel to the road.
The feathery, flexible branchlets
Fashion an enchanting spectacle
Oozing ecstasy;
Crows alight
And fly off again.
Walking along the level pavement
Of the long straight road
With the breeze on my face
And the sun weakened by cloud,
I look out to sea—
The green rippling waves,
The boats sauntering around,
The dark hills on the horizon.

Tamarind

This tree near the gate
Of my garden growing effulgently
Constitutes a cynosure
To not a few passersby,
Not on account of its fragrant flowers,
Yellow sepals, and red-veined petals,
Not on account of its delicate leaves
That fold together in the dusk,
But by virtue of its ginger-brown pods
Enclosing seeds covered with green edible pulp.
In they ambulate and pluck them—
Some ask for permission,
But the majority don't.

Rambutan

No exalted height boasts the tree
Or pronounced girth its trunk;
The spreading branches
Fumble an untidy mass;
Beauty does not permeate it,
Nor any distinction impress its seal.

But when the green unripe fruits
Mature into crimson bunches
Of ellipsoids with long soft hairs,
They wear a captivating mien.

Pluck a glowing specimen
And squeeze open the rind;
Admire the thick creamy aril,
Which can be stripped clean off the seed,
And revel in its sweet taste—
Most delicious of fruits!

No rapture is evoked by tree,
But when the fruiting season comes
It grows an agreeable spectacle
In spite of silent turmoil of black ants,
Which relish it even more than man.

Airport

Once an unruffled expanse of land
Distant from the city streets,
Sun-drenched fields alive with grain,
And farmers stolidly tending them—
It now gyrates a busier scene.

Gray buildings huddle on the site:
Control tower with glass walls,
Hangars and warehouses,
Air-conditioned passenger terminal
With its diverse sections—
Customs, immigration, ticket counters,
Restaurant, lounge, duty-free shops.

The grounds are paved with tracks,
With runways and taxiways,
Operating areas constituting
The terra firma of the aircraft
Traversing the skyways.

From the horizon approaches a plane,
From a runway a jet rises;
From all over the world
Come the mechanical eagles
In obstreperous flight,
A continual stream
Of takeoffs and landings.

For the passengers arises the motley scene,
People of many races and nationalities,
Jostling, sitting, standing;
Baggage of all shapes and sizes
Careers down the conveyor belts
Or lies stacked in heaps.

Modern material civilization
With its restless activity,
Its fusillade of noise,
Its impatient speed,
Its shrinkage of the world,
Finds its symbol
In the airport with its planes.

Sauntering at Midnight

Night rates better than day
For peace and thought;
In the lingering silence
The mind discards its fardel
And gambols in freedom and bliss.

Midnight and I am sauntering alone
Along this country road;
Above, the moon in her third quarter
And an assemblage of vague stars,
Half the sky away,
Looking disconsolately at her waxing power.

The heavenly bodies distil
Slightly less mystery and remoteness
Than they did in times past;
Spacecraft have flown to the planets,
And astronauts have landed on the moon,
But as erewhile
They display to us on earth
Tableau of circles and specks of light.

To the left rises a plantation
Of coconut palms whose silhouettes
Dangle in the air;
Sleep stupefies the abodes
In the neighbourhood.

On the right, vacant land
Exhales gloom and desolation;
Away in the distance
The scattered lights of bungalows
Gaze from high land.

Silence, the fisherman,
Has spread his effectual net
And caught all the fish of sound;
Silence is beautiful,
And the silence of midnight
Is the most glamorous.

Virtus Post Nummos

The proboscis of interest nowadays
Follows mainly the scent of money,
The major study, the pregnant key
To the ideal life, is economics,
Violent revolutions and more violent wars
Are terroristic preludes to material betterment.

One endowed with normality
And luxuriant with good sense
First sets out to ferret a fortune
By legally right modes or wrong,
Then if he enjoys the flavour
Of admiration from his fellows,
He blossoms into a philanthropist
Performing complacent donations.

Workers gather in militant aggregations,
Their weapon the temporary cessation
Of the activities for which they are hired,
Their motivation to secure
More money for less work;
Their talk rotates unweariedly
On the axis of the cost of living.

Tan Kheng Yeang

Industrialists have their vision glued
To profits streaming from their companies,
The ethics buzzing in their actions
Is business ethics, accepted commercial practice,
Aimed at target of efficiency
In the acquisition of money;
Virtue per se if at all discernible
Is but a faint speck
On their guiding map of life.

Money has never sat an autocrat
Of such stupendous puissance before,
Nor has virtue ever taken
So skulking a second place,
Not even striding close
But limping far in the rear.

Queues

A sweltering string of oars along the road
Backward stretches from the entrance to the ferry;
Fifteen minutes for the steamer to scuttle through
The one-mile expanse of water
And two hours for a vehicle before
It may roll fretfully onto its deck.

From the lobby of the cinema
The queues extend right to the pavement,
Patiently tarrying to hook tickets—
Cannot the show be tossed away?

Walk past the general post office
And view the lines at the diverse counters
Desirous of purchasing stamps,
Registering letters for fear of loss,
Sending or cashing money orders.

The queue is the order of the day
For dissipating time and life;
Can measures not be contrived
To deracinate this phenomenon?
Or is it a fascinating spectacle?

Tan Kheng Yeang

Noise Everywhere

Wherever we find ourselves
Noise hovers in the vicinity,
Persistent, hideous, exasperating,
A demon revelling in the air.

It pounds in the streets,
Slithering from the human voice
And tread of human feet,
Somersaulting from the streams of motor vehicles;
Grass-cutting machines on side tables and lawns
Shoot agony through the atmosphere.

Make your way to a factory
And confront the whirr of machinery,
And you will wish the Industrial Age
Had never stepped into being;
Saunter into an office
And hear the ringing of telephones
Linked to the din of speech.

Not only in the anthills of population,
But in rural areas too,
Noise castigates the scene;
Distortion of perception to fancy
That the lowing of cows
Or the croaking of frogs
Is a display of Nature's music;
The ubiquitous car rumbles through it,
And precipitately comes the raucous train.

Noise disdains to cling to the ground.
It must soar high into the air
In the company of airplanes,
It must sail on the sea
With steamers and motorboats;
Noise vibrates sovereign of the world.

Symbol

Everything can stand a symbol
Of some other entity,
It's just a point of fancy;
The sun is a symbol of energy,
The moon of gentleness,
The cloud of vagueness;
Mercury is a symbol of fickleness
And lead of dullness;
The flower is a symbol of beauty,
The eagle of majesty;
Handshaking is a symbol of friendship.
Symbolism smirks a facile tool
For the texturing of romance;
It is a reprehensible practice
When exercised to excess,
As in rites and ceremonies;
It's better to apprehend things
As they breathe in actuality
Instead of through the haze
Of imaginative representation.

Tan Kheng Yeang

To Dream and Fail

It's better of some lofty achievement to dream
And reach not to net it
Than to tread the road of life
Gazing at prosaic trivia;
To be invested with an ideal
Is to fit the mind with wings,
To make it soar through the universe.
He who is captive to his environment,
Deeming his paltry concerns
Grasp the sum of things,
Is not to be strewn with admiration
As one relishing the bliss of contentment.
A seemingly illusory ambition
Merits not supercilious disdain
As a fatuous fantasy;
An elevated aim without fruition
Is not divested of its sublimity.
The success of failure
Irradiates the intellectual mind;
Leave the failure of success
To the vulgar, the petty.
Let us dream, and if we fail,
Let us fail with pride;
A great plan remains great.

Utility

Utility grins the test of a product,
It registers comfort
And physical well-being,
It spells the objective
Of a material civilization,
It glows a need of life;
Irrational to reject it,
To deem it of base grain,
To condemn it in the name of spiritual greatness
Or superiority of aesthetic values.
But the exaggeration of it,
Trumpeting it into the sole criterion,
This is asinine, noxious.
Utility is an instrument,
Not the target of existence;
It is the foundation
Of a tolerable life
Not its summum bonum,
Not its pinnacle of glory.

The State

What aura engirdles the state
That it should transcend its members?
Nothing but an organization
To net certain objectives,
It should not parade omnipotence
Or haul worship as though sacred;
It stands just a utilitarian device
For the benefit of its components.

Naught screams more of the ridiculous
Than for one person or a clique
To identify itself with the state
And impound its members
In the corral of absolute rule;
No justification can breathe for this.

Strange indeed the majority
Can tolerate an individual
Lay tyrannous hands on them;
If their support does not flow
In active or passive stream,
The absolutist could not bray his might.

People lean towards admiration of personalities
And easily bow their minds to power;
This queer infirmity is accountable
For the success and prevalence of despotism.

Hero worship is an insidious peril
When it revolves round force;
This abject trait seemingly innocuous
Should be contemned and eradicated;
The only rational reaction
A dictator should educe
Is fervid opposition.

Mentally Conquered

The worst shape of defeat
Is defeat of the mind;
One may be constrained to succumb
To superior force,
But this external capitulation
Is not so abject
As mental acceptance.

The mind is the last fortress of freedom;
To surrender this from any cause
Is ignominious insolvency of sense;
Mentally to come to terms
With the triumphant despot
And deem his ways and measures right
Is to sink in the quagmire of servility.

To accede to social forces
And think as others do
Is only one step less inglorious
Than relishing oligarchic sway;
The strong is adamantine in his ideas
And hugs his freedom of thought,
Repudiating in his mind
A tyrant's blandishments and threats
Or society's attachments and aversions;
One may have to yield outwardly
But need not acquiesce inwardly.

Diverse are the forces
Endeavouring to bake the dough of thought
And ferment the wine of action:
Direct physical violence,
Coercion operated by the law,
The pressure of social opinion,
Constraint of economic factors,
Bombardment by propaganda;
To remain mentally unconquered
And confide in authentic reason
Is a veritable achievement.

Welfare of the People

The welfare of the people
Is what every government
Perspires to meliorate or feigns;
But what constitutes welfare?
Is it personal happiness
On a material plane?
Is it moral rectitude
According to some specific code?
Is it liberty, equality, fraternity?
Or the greatest happiness
Of the greatest number of people?
Or is it synonymous with
The greatness of the state?
Or is it proletarian solidarity?
The welfare of the people
Gyrates a vague concept,
A glib expression on the tongues
Of rulers and of politicians,
A facade for cant—
In its name strange things are done
Antithetic to it.

Originality

Originality throughout past ages sidled
A figure of scorn;
He who preached a new idea
Or discovered a strange product
Or behaved in a unique way
Evoked ridicule as an eccentric
Or contumely as a fool
Or dread as a lunatic
Or prosecution as a criminal.

In truth it's singular all people
Should have arrived to trot
Along the same platform of behaviour;
This phenomenon blazons the efficiency
Of social pressure and the imitative faculty;
Instead of the rule,
Originality stands the exception;
Titanic strength of character
And elevated level of intelligence
Are the concomitants for it
To survive in a social context.

Nowadays it appears a reputable trait,
Eulogized a radiant gift;
But does it lure true admiration?
The genuinely original
Is hardly less contemned than before
It hauls praise only after it has become
Fashionable and shed its uniqueness;
What is glorified with the epithet
Is often some slight variation,
Not too commonly found,
Of some conventional entity
Or just its development to high degree.

The authentic originator
Is not he who breathes
The incense of fame;
Rather it's the developer
Or the populariser who nets success,
And even he has to wade
Through the mud of ignorance and prejudice
For many distressful years.

News

Avidity for news
Screams the loudest human trait;
When one encounters another,
They trade information
About their friends and acquaintances
And what has saluted their eyes and ears.

The greatest purveyor of intelligence
Is the omnipresent newspaper
That diurnally echoes events
From all corners of the globe—
Earthquakes and volcanoes,
Floods and droughts,
Robberies and murders,
Riots and wars,
Actions and plans of governments.

News is the food of curiosity—
The spicier the tastier;
Violent phenomena, tragic events,
And scandals magnetize wrong attention.
What else does it evince?
Interest in the world;
This, if of wholesome character,
Could not extract dismay—
Desirable to have knowledge of affairs
And the phenomena of the world.

Illusion

We reside in illusion.
Reality impinging on our minds
Makes us sense phenomena
Which representing distort it.
We see a sky
Where no entity is;
We see twinkling specks of stars
That surpass the earth in size;
We see vacant space
Between one object and another,
Space rollicking with air.
Every race deems its typical features
As constituting the norm of beauty;
Every people hears its language
As a mellifluous stream of sound;
The dress in fashion
Looks eminently attractive;
The ideas one grows up with
Are naturally correct;
We avow as inherently right
The current patterns of behaviour;
Whatever is strange
shocks and is unacceptable.
We fabricate a realm of illusion
And dub it real.

The Wind

When it blows softly,
Playfully lifting the leaves
Or bending the flowers,
What allurement it exudes!
When it flies wildly,
Roaring in obstreperous anger,
Uprooting trees and tossing debris,
What affright it discharges!
An amorphous mystery,
Symbol of soft strength,
Still silent air
Becomes a flowing garrulous current;
We feel what we didn't,
Might revels where none was manifest.
I love the wind,
Be it breeze or hurricane,
Ineffable, invisible
Flowing force,
Singing as it rolls.

Waiting for Train

Here at the railway station
I wait for the express
To puff in from Singapore;
Down the night whisper numerous stars,
Around still and hot stands the air;
I sit on a bench and read
Or stroll along the lengthy platform.

Scheduled for 9:10 PM,
On my reaching Butterworth,
Its time had metamorphosed to 9:35;
An announcement struts unabashed—
The train is delayed
And will only arrive at 9:50;
Impatience scampers through my mind;
What inefficiency coils round this service?

The clock has now jogged to 10:00,
And no sound of a train is audible
And no further announcement either;
Wrath is gathering a storm;
Abruptly my serenity returns,
I drop on the bench and reflect—
Why the surge of impatience?
Why should trains bear punctuality's label?
Is an hour or so of such import?
Away with all hurry and disquiet—
Life is a concoction of trifles.

Tan Kheng Yeang

Never Such Danger

Never such danger
Hissed in the world before;
A savage twinkling in the jungle
Might terminate inside a tiger;
But what is that
Compared to the diurnal snares
Woven by the spider of traffic?
Death crouches in the air or on the road.

The warriors of olden times
Tossed ferocity with sword or arrow,
And a Temujin or Tamerlane
Rode over fields of corpses;
But what is that
Compared to the demented nuclear bomb
That could depopulate the earth?
The vaunted civilized age of today
Is the haunt of violent death.

Ruins

This house has rambled through a century;
Ruin has it in its grasp;
The tiled roof cries with huge orifices,
The brick walls stand uneasily,
The wooden upper floor has shrieked into nothingness,
The various rooms have blended into one;
Spiders throw their nets around.

House and man need each other;
Man is the mind of house;
People resided here before
And circulated life to the place;
Children scampered and played,
And adults worked and fretted;
What joys and sorrows
Has this building stared at?

Did only one family breathe here,
Or were there several in succession?
What were their vicissitudes?
Some members have faded from life;
What has befallen the survivors?
Everybody grips an interesting history.

All things wear the ephemeral label—
House and man alike;
No decay engenders a sadder sight
Than a dilapidated building;
In Nature, material deterioration
Merely spells transformation;
With human habitations
It resembles organic death.

Division Three

Routine

day after day in the office
seated at the same table
grasping the same pen
encumbered with similar chores
solving similar problems
conversing with the same personnel
encountering strangers with similar interests

curious how habit
makes for acceptance
even enjoyment of the monotonous
the meaningless
but then habit itself
the routine of behaviour
a case of one routine accommodating another

routine of behaviour
routine of work
creatures of routine
whether we are incarcerated
in an office or not
only difference
the meticulous red tape
spells the dullest of routines

consequence of routine
fuming and fretting
and yearning to flee
come some catastrophe
be it war
or personal misadventure
then about-face of thought
so secure tranquil comfortable
our former routine
gleams the acme of the desirable
so strange the human mind

Motorcycle

as a suicidal contrivance
nothing to beat the motorcycle
blithely purring along
when a dog scampers across the street
or a cyclist swerves towards a junction
collision
scatheless the other party
dead the poor motorcyclist
other than fatal accidents galore
a fractured spine
a mutilated limb
a twisted neck
a broken head
a lacerated face
a damaged brain
a sightless eye

an unstable vehicle
with the speed of the robust
riders at a reckless age
collecting thrills
as connoisseurs antiques
what a triumphant combination
for carnage and death
what a homicidal invention

Brickwork

argillaceous earth
moulded into oblong shape
fired in a kiln
plasticity off
and rigidity on
hardness and durability

vigorous red bricks
convenient for handling
disposed in regular courses
to uprear a wall
bedded and bonded
in cement mortar

stretchers and headers
fraternizing into an array
compact homogeneous
of symmetrical form
stable firm
bearing the required loading
small units fashioning a large mass
an admirable army of stalwart individuals

Foundations

below the ground
pits of regular dimensions
cement concrete
of requisite thickness
deposited and compacted

a necessity
otherwise fracture
of walls if reared
direct on ground
of variable strength
inviting uneven settlement

bases wider
than walls supported
to distribute load
over sensible area

foundations to forestall
failure of structures
designed to cope
with bearing strength of soil
clay sand gravel rock
small masses of matter
shouldering much bulkier loads
a noteworthy phenomenon

Traffic Signs

everywhere traffic signs
a veritable forest
so abundant that
they get scant respect

inverted triangle in a circle
stop look go
to stop and look
when traffic is sparse
temptation irresistible
to ignore it

parking prohibited
cars allowed to move
but unable to park
almost every street
luxuriantly displaying
the red circles
with red diagonals
what a task
endeavouring to secure
a place of rest

no entry
awesome the number
of one-way streets
going round and round
to attain a destination
red disks with white horizontals
what a minatory look

keep left
conceded that one
should travel on the left
but without the presence
of the blue rectangular plate
and the words in white clarity
more convenient to use
the middle or the right
at a junction

dangerous bend
road intersection
pedestrian crossing
uneven road
the red border triangles
what a wearisome horde

other than the signs
the white lines on the roads
what about traffic lights
with their green amber red
roundabouts and overpasses
subways and overhead bridges

this complexity
the price paid
for the employment of
the motor vehicle
but still ineffectual
accidents gripping injuries
and deaths
diurnal occurrences

Environmental Pollution

thus of industrial
and domestic wastes
sewage oil detergents
chemicals and solid refuse
pouring into the rivers and seas
bacteriological contamination
water exhausted of oxygen

noxious fumes and gases
injected into the atmosphere
in baleful quantities
injurious to health
from factories
from moving motor vehicles

how to bridle pollution
ominous that science
foresees not a problem
only wrestling with it
when precipitately it alights
in a frightful tangle

objective to control environment
and mould of it a better place
for human habitation
not to pollute it
but scientific progress
ever thus
good with evil in tow
still what science produces
science to unravel

The Arch

a structure in form of a curve
support of a bridge above
or wall of building over an opening
of stone or brick or reinforced concrete
array of wedge-shaped voussoirs
pressing against and supporting one another
bed joints normal to curve
springers resting on piers
strongly resistant to arch thrust
admirable work of stone
more beautiful than anything straight
of structures the most captivating
an arched bridge over flowing water
artistic part of landscape
a row of arches forming arcade
conferring aesthetic look on a building

Tan Kheng Yeang

The Culvert

small river
curving its unenthusiastic way along
steep banks
triumphant with green grass
whole year round
this country road
of asphalt macadam
intersecting it
at right angles
traversing it
on the back of a culvert
four galvanized metal pipes
befriended by a foundation
of cement concrete
this culvert without charm
unabashedly utilitarian
beauty desirable
in every existent thing
more so for structures
compassed to endure

Air

hollow sphere palpitating round the earth
invisible mixture of mainly
oxygen and nitrogen
but presence detectable
tactilely and experimentally
material air seemingly immaterial

from air to wind
a matter of movement
symbol of unsuspected strength
soft cool breeze
dallying with leaves and flowers
violent storm deracinating trees
giant gone berserk

essential for life
even more than water and food
a solitary ingredient
to serve this purpose
odd that this element
should react to compose a gas
inimical to animal organisms
such the character of nature

Water

wrapped in mantle of water
three-fourths of the globe
in form of oceans
symbol of adaptability
flowing round land
and fashioning coves gulfs bays

even on land
water exuberant
everywhere rivers and waterfalls
ponds and lakes
rain in drizzles and showers

infiltrating the ground
progress barricaded by impermeable clay
oozing into wells
bursting as springs

water quiescent
or in flux
its daedal pattern
for the imagination

beauty of water
in the blue of oceans
and the green of lakes
in the fall of rain
and the flight of snow
in the waves of the sea
and the unrest of the river

music of water
in the cadence of waves
and the murmur of brooks
in the splash of rain
and the roar of cataracts various and glamorous
the sound of water

Steam

elevation of temperature
metamorphosis of water to steam
gliding away into atmosphere
hot and smoky
symbol of effervescent zeal
sun gazing on the sea
vapour swinging into the sky
formation of glamorous cloud
floating in serene beauty
glooming amorphous masses
and tumbling rain
thaumaturgic power
a frail substance
puissant to propel turbines
trains and ships

Ice

declension of temperature
transformation of water into ice
cold and glittering
symbol of hard purity
a solid but unlike most
committed to irresolution
balancing on the weather
or degree of cold
pendent icicles from eaves
pearls of frost on flowers
buoyant icebergs in the ocean
clattering hail volleying from the skies
expansion of volume
and pummelling open of pipes
reinforcement with salt
and shrinking down of freezing point
amazing the phenomena of change

Electricity

indecipherable entity
shot with wondrous properties
visible as lightning
but for human purposes
imprisoned in copper wires

an electric circuit
a closed continuous circle
of conducting matter
with a source of supply
a dynamo or battery
and accoutred with switch
for making or breaking it

potent to magnetize
steel and nickel and cobalt
operating on principle of electromagnetism
cranes to elevate weighty loads
bells to excite attention

electric energy to flash light
to whirl cooling fans
to radiate heat for ironing
to stimulate cookers
to drive vehicles
to vitalize machinery
the modern utilitarian miracle

Sound

vibrations of object
engendering waves in the atmosphere
percussing the ear
similar vibrations
and sound the result

velocity of sound
a crawl compared to lights
serviceable for calculating distance
as of cliff
from ship at sea

sonic buffetings
on reflecting surfaces
like hills and walls
and echoes the acknowledgment
dulcet the reverberation
from a single sound

the zenith of sound
the glamour of music
but not because of the intimate knowledge
of relationship of pitch to frequency
loudness to amplitude of vibration

the nadir of sound
the discordance of noise
nondescript raucous
some natural mostly artificial
its elimination
an unequivocal boon
still for acoustics to encompass

Retaining Wall

of reinforced concrete or masonry
raised to forestall disintegration
of earth bank from weathering
to arrest its sliding action

to survive in equilibrium
repose of earth at certain angle
according to its nature and moisture content
if earth mass fairly vertical
pressure inflicted by unstable wedge
on structure in front

monolithic mass of wall
of adequate thickness against thrust
if fashioned with vertical or battered face
and sloping back
economical effective symbol
of human structure
combating natural force

Hydrogen

lightest of gases
lightest of elements
invisible elf
bare of colour taste smell
on tiptoe to burst into blue flame
devoid of illumination

devoted affinity for oxygen
with which it fashions water
sodium potassium or calcium
in water and hydrogen floats out
hydrogen over a metallic oxide
reduction to water and metal

some uses of the gas
dilatation of balloons
transformation of oils into solids
production of motor spirits
manufacture of ammonia

so imponderous the element
so innocuous it seems
yet the heinous bomb
awesome release of energy
from conversion of nuclei
of hydrogen to helium ones

Iron

most estimable of metals
silver-hued magnetic ductile malleable
basic need of civilization
eminent material of structures
of productive machinery
of tools most useful and most used

reduction of natural ores
mixtures of iron oxides
and clay silica or other earthy material
ores like magnetite haematite
limonite siderite
pig iron the fruit from which
derive diverse varieties of metal

feverish with elevated temperature
in blast furnace smelting
in company of flux
most commonly limestone
yield of slag
separable from the metal

solid fuel coal coke charcoal
to donate heat for liquefaction
and the chemical reactions
and to perform as reducing agent
exiling oxygen from the oxide
in form of gas

cast iron high in carbon
hard brittle melting easily
redoubtable for columns and struts
to combat compressive stress
and attractive for numerous products
like pipes gratings and machine parts
in that it can cheaply assume
complex forms protean-like

wrought iron almost bereft
of all entangling carbon
soft ductile malleable weldable
gifted with tenacity
worthy foe of tension
useful for wire and ornamental work

sovereign of all iron
steel with moderate hug of carbon
variously hardened by tempering
strong tenacious elastic
fusible forgeable ductile
mild steel for bridges girders trusses
hard steel for cutting tools

release of different sounds
cast iron muffled tone
wrought iron response of low pitch
steel glorious treble ring
structure of cast iron crystalline
of wrought iron fibrous
of steel granular

admirable the ingenuity of man
in utilization of natures bounty
development of resources
a task meriting pursuit
for progress of products
ceaseless experimentation a necessity

Tan Kheng Yeang

Magnet

a truly gripping wonder the magnet
an unpretentious bar of iron
in appearance not deviating from stolid others
but strange its properties

an article brought into contact
of iron cobalt or nickel
and it clings like print to paper
or as though fatuously in love
adhering not to any segment
but to an extremity

iron filings tossed
over magnetic field
and emergence of a pattern
round the magnet
along the lines of force

attraction of north pole of one magnet
for south pole of another
but repulsion for its north
like to unlike and not like to like
antithesis of human characteristic

odd when caressed by a magnet
to find a humdrum splinter of steel
transform into one itself
or when in vicinity of electric current
become an electromagnet

a rod of the metal
set to oscillate at fancy
and it dwindles to rest
in one favoured position
immovably the same
what munificent bounty to voyagers
the invention of the compass

strange the glories of nature
but its beauties of form and hue
no comparison to
the hypnotic charm of its properties

Paint

a composite material
pigment and base
dissolved in vehicle
pigment the powdery beauty
bestowing the requisite hue
derivation from organic
earthy or metallic sources
substance like ochre sienna
umber or lampblack

base the principal constituent
determinant of paints durability
such as iron oxide zinc white
red or white lead
vehicle the desiccant liquid
reading story of paint
in even tones
for durable work oil
commonly linseed oil

filler to correct weight
and curtail expense
substances like gypsum and barytes
drier entering scene prior to use
to urge paints drying
litharge an example

resort to a brush
to release the fluid
on surfaces of buildings
woodwork and ironwork
congealing into impervious coating
a shield against weathering
an ornamental appearance

mode of exterior beautification
concealing repellent drabness
to scamper off after a time
symbol of superficial attraction
of no lasting value
extrinsic to subject

Glass

sodium or potassium silicate
in intimate fusion
with oxide of calcium or lead
resultant glass
an amorphous substance
poor conductor of electricity

plastic mass for moulding at red heat
transparent hard and brittle when cooled
variation in composition
for glass of different kinds
manganese to breed whiteness
oxide of a metal for colour
potash and lead to sparkle lustrous
boric oxide for heat resistance

sheet glass of diverse thicknesses
less than quarter inch
fabricated with natural surface
of molten material
cut with diamond for glazing
capable of opacity by grinding

plate glass of thicknesses
up to an inch
and of striking amplitude
cast on smooth iron table
rolled ground and polished

fashioned into mirrors and lenses
tiles and windowpanes
covers for pictures and cabinets
bottles and drinking vessels
electric bulbs and tubes

beautiful delightful
whether plain or hued
of substances unique
in its perfect transparency
an enchanting invention
of olden time
comparable to the best
of modern days

Granite

igneous acid rook
fashioned by volcanic wrath
in deep concealment
beneath terrestrial integument
consolidated from molten passion

blasting of the plutonic rock
with its elevated percentage of silica
into impressive blocks
which may be squared and worked
for alluring ashlar masonry
or chewed by crusher into chips
and spit out graded in various sizes

light in hue usually gray
in structure granular and crystalline
drinking but little water
hard strong resistant to weather
a composition of quartz
mica and feldspar
and possibly hornblende
magnetite and zircon

utilization in buildings
for walling and columns
in bridges for abutments and arches
for roads as blocks or macadam
as aggregates in concrete

felicitous gift of nature
serviceable with no modification
of its character its properties
finest of stones
for structural works
worthy of hymn of praise

Concrete

a glory of fabrication
mixture of inert substances
adhering by the magic of water
to awake a sturdy compact
durable homogeneous material
for yield of good concrete
dense strong resistant
unalterable uniform
intimate commingling of ingredients
frolicking in a revolving drum
deposition of plastic mass
without angry segregation
intense compaction to maximum density
sympathetic curing by control
of temperature and moisture
removal of formwork after adequate hardening
a process of chemical change

numerous the factors
fingering quality and strength
degree of control
hinged to nature of work
and vindicable cost

elite of coarse aggregates granite
graded of diverse sizes
fine aggregate sharp coarse sand
divorced from impurities
gluey agent portland cement
of standard specification
fresh pure water
in quantity just potable by mix

quantitative relationships
of cement sand and stone
cement to block all voids in sand
mortar to choke all interstices in stone
strength of concrete a distillation
of amount of cement
optimum measure for greatest strength
and on water cement ratio

this wondrous product of control
a gift for all construction
walls and foundations of buildings
pavements and roads
retaining walls and bridges
dams and reservoirs

Aluminium

as commercial metal
specific to twentieth century
strange this when in abundance
it struts third among the elements
sprung from bauxite and cryolite
malleable ductile noncorrosive
light metal forming alloys
suffused with notable strength
low electrical resistance
admirable conductor of heat
yet as fine reflector
utilizable for heat insulation
use in form of
drawn rolled or cast metal
foil or powder
for transmission lines
for domestic appliances
in printing explosives and paint

Asphalt

bitumen clasping torpid mineral matter
evolved by nature
in pitch lakes and bituminous rocks
or fabricated by man
bitumen from distillation of coal or petroleum
commingled with a calcareous or siliceous compound
durable tough noiseless
valorous antagonist of water
fire and weather
softening to touch of heat
spread easily and without seams
gracefully flexible to accommodate movement
of service for buildings
setting into impervious mass
when covering roofs and floors
or in damp-proof courses
admirable for formation of road surface
and lining tanks and reservoirs
type of natural product
human ingenuity turns to advantage

Light

light for the earth
principal fount the sun
stream of energy
flying at incredible speed
with transverse wave motion through space

light landing on an object
reflection and it is visible
the darker the material the less shot back
total absorption by black surface
resplendent racing through
transparent glass and water

rays in straight lines
from source that kicks light in all directions
but course perforce bent
when light twinkles from one medium
to another as from air to water
such refraction only
when kissing new surface at oblique angle

effect of refraction
shimmering landscape on hot day
straight rod appearing flexed upwards in water
pond looking a quarter less than real depth
use of refraction
microscope and telescope
spectacles and camera

beam of white light
a bundle of varied rays procreating diverse colours
running of sunlight through glass prism
dispersion to display spectrum
of hues of the rainbow
odd that reflection of certain rays
should give an entity its complexion

light breathing visibility into phenomena
without its magic world might as well not be
so far as humans are concerned
light the revealer of matter

Carbon

element at acme of significance
though a mere fraction of one percent
of stuff composing earths crust
breathing pure as diamond bright hard jewel
and graphite dark soft mineral

fraternizing with other substances this metalloid
in form of petroleum and coal
or as carbonates mainly of calcium
shouting in hills of limestone rock
enamouringly strange the stalactites and stalagmites in caves

in air as carbon dioxide
so benevolent to plants
with aid of sunlight decomposition
into carbon retained and oxygen released
so malevolent to animals
which only expire it as waste product

basis of vegetable and animal matter
bridge between animate and inanimate realms
striking ability of this atom
for sharing electrons with others
fruit numerous complex organic compounds
glory to carbon
lifes distinctive element

Clouds

transformation into vapour
of water on sea and land
caressed by heat of sun
its ascent in the troposphere
into the upper colder region
where it condenses into clouds
masses of water droplets
formation of various types at diverse heights
scanning from upper to lower atmosphere
cirrus looking down on others from its lofty height
though consisting of white feathery wisps of puny size
making halos with its ice crystals
round sun and moon
cirrocumulus appearing as small white ripply flocks or specks
cirrostratus with thin disarranged sheets
altostratus displaying tangled webs
wearing a watery look
altocumulus large slightly globular heaps
harbouring tiny drops of water
cumulonimbus of gigantic magnitude
rising from low to great height
harbinger of thunder and lightning
prevalent in tropical regions
nimbus amorphous dark masses
which shoot down rain
cumulus of vertical structure
with level base and curved head
and white or gray in hue
stratocumulus screening the heavens
with its rolling globular masses
stratus low above ground
uniform stretch of wide extent
appearing like floating fog
beauty resident in clouds
whether heaped or stratiform in shape
whether white black or lit by sunlight
to golden or crimson
whether floating with fleet grace
or shifting in slumberous gravity
all this a product of the transmuting wand of nature

Lithosphere

structure of earth
mainly a hot liquid core
wrapped in a solid mantle
then the hard shell
the lithosphere of rocky material
incomparably less in thickness

crust of two layers
the sial the continental crust
rich in silica and alumina
discontinuous principally of granite rocks
overlying a continuous envelope of heavier basalt
the sima constituting ocean floors
luxuriant with silica and magnesia

nexus of continental level
via continental slope
with ocean floor level
continental surface rugged
with mountains plateaus and plains
irregular too the ocean floor
with its ridges deeps and basins

earth movements generating
vertical and lateral displacement
successive rock layers
plicated and fractured
parts of bottom strata
propelled upward
and the superficial
squeezed vertical or inclined

entanglement of our minds
in a web of awe
when contemplating the tremendous forces
moulding the home of life

Heat

form of energy
susceptible to interchangeability
with other varieties
rooted in conservation of energy
equivalent quantities involved

power of transformation
of state of physical body
from solid to liquid
or liquid to gas
heat instrumental in the change
without variation of temperature
striking this the phenomenon of latent heat

nexus of temperature
to quantity of heat
but for diverse substances
different amounts enlisted
to raise identical masses
through same range of temperature
to every substance its specific heat

transference of heat
conduction when heat walks
from particle to adjacent particle as in solid
convection when heated portion
swims to colder haven as in liquid
radiation when heat flies
in form of electromagnetic waves as from sun

expansion of solids with heat
though small the amount
correction imperative as in balance wheel of watch
expansion of liquids as of mercury
utilitarian thermometer
expansion of gases most spectacular
variation of volume directly as temperature
provided pressure stands still

thermal energy the eventual outcome
of all categories of energy
flow of heat naturally
from hot to cold body
ultimately universe at one temperature
and all energy defunct

Nitrogen

a diatomic stable inactive gas
living pure in atmosphere
of which it flows four-fifths
inconsiderably lighter than air
sans colour smell or taste
not flammable not agent of combustion

combined nitrogen a sine qua non of all life
a constituent of proteins forming protoplasm
nitrogen drunk by plants
from solutions of nitrates in soil
and eaten by animals and humans
in form of proteins from substance of organisms

odd the nitrogen cycle
atmospheric nitrogen
rendered usable by plants
through instrumentality of lightning or bacteroids
forging by plants of proteins
consumed by animals
which expel part as waste
whence nitrogen compounds produced in soil
finally through action of bacteria
nitrogen released back to atmosphere

serviceable principally in such compounds
as ammonia nitric acid or ammonium salts
materials utilized in manufacture
of explosives and fertilizers
dyes pharmaceuticals and plastics
strange the products an element can generate

Sodium

silvery metallic element
so soft as to be sliced with ease
lower in density than water
burning with scintillating golden flame
obliging heat and electricity
too reactive for free existence
unhesitatingly oxidizing in air
capable of shattering water
with evolution of hydrogen and intense heat

one of elements in richest profusion
compounds in wide distribution
dragging some of these out to view
and leaving unnamed the numerous others

wonderful sodium chloride
familiar table salt
weighty constituent of food
teeming in land and sea
industrial fountain of sodium and its other compounds

sodium hydroxide alias caustic soda
a white crystalline solid
readily making extremely potent soluble base
decomposing action on fats
of greatest import among industrial alkalis
useful for manufacture of soap
and mercerization of cotton

sodium carbonate one of few soluble carbonates
dissolution of anhydrous salt
in hot water and a decahydrate
washing soda floats into existence
serviceable for softening water
and in manufacture of glass

admirable that man can transform
every material for his benefit
ingenuity and exertion needed
alas the day that they fail

Trigonometry

odd that an entire science
should glide round the properties
of one figure the triangle
the relations exuding
from its sides and angles
a figure of three sharp corners
and nursing a right angle
the ratio of every two sides
and six float into view
sine cosine tangent
cosecant secant cotangent
for each size of angle
constant the value
irrelevant the lengths of lines
amazing that these trigonometric functions
should pinch such import
and strange the array of formulae arising
results of practical interest possible
determination of width of river
or height of hill
or gradient of road
a tribute to human ingenuity
this notable performance of reason

Weathering

the forces of the atmosphere
formidable agents of change
seemingly soft and nerveless
but diabolic in their obstinate strength
their orgy of destruction
relentless through aeons
continuous denudation of masses of land
disintegration of rocks
production of soil

influential the pendulum of temperature
expansion of rocks with heat in daytime
their contraction with lively radiation at night
effect of such ceaseless strains
decortication and cleaving of superficial areas
like impairment of face of cliff

imbibing of gases by descending rain
use to oxidize substances
or generate carbonates
thus releasing cohesion of particles
on surfaces of rocks
which disintegration makes its own

development of frost
from water trapped in ground
richer space demanded by ice
so forcible kicking apart of components
on thawing of frozen mass
earth or mud the sequel

strange the results of the inexorable forces
transformation of topography of globe
corrosion of soft material
while hard parts remain arrogant
fairly even land
shuddering into hills and ridges
valleys and ravines
curious shapes of rock
and tortuous caves and tunnels
sand dunes moulded by wind
and rivers lakes and springs fashioned by rain
truly momentous the changes
nudged through geologic time

Tan Kheng Yeang

Copper

dense soft malleable metal
so ductile it can be drawn thinner than hair
unreactive resistant to corrosion
exalted melting and boiling points
transcendent conductor of heat and electricity
base metal to the alchemists
one of greatest import in industry
fairly abundant this reddish element
familiar from prehistoric days

easily reducible ores
an oxide like cuprite
a carbonate like malachite
a sulphide like chalcopyrite
heating with coke to strip cuprite to copper
and malachite to cuprite thence copper
heating of chalcopyrite with restriction of air
and copper sulphide struts free
part of which becomes cuprite
further heating of the sulphide and oxide
and copper comes to view

source of bundle of alloys
commingled with nickel to build monel
with zinc brass
with tin bronze
special brasses and bronzes fabricated
by admixture of third element
like phosphorus aluminium silicon
odd the successor to the stone age
should have been the era of an alloy
instead of simply a single metal

easily moulded into wire
much in demand for transmission of electricity
for which extreme purity vital
employed for ornaments or coins
for water piping or cooking utensils
numerous the uses of its alloys
like brass for cartridges hardware and musical instruments

Chlorine

a gaseous transparent element
a halogen of yellowish green hue
in existence as diatomic covalent molecules
heavy asphyxiating
poisonous germicidal
not recalcitrant to solution in water
willingly submissive to liquefaction

hungry affinity for hydrogen
happily removing it
hence magnificent oxidizing agent
invested with restless activity
reacting with most elements
to fashion chlorides
a commercially useful trait

not floating free in nature
locked in principal salts of sea
found in alliance with such metals
as sodium potassium magnesium and calcium
commercial chlorine mainly
from electrolysis of brine
some part from oxidation of hydrogen chloride

for bleaching in paper and textile industries
for sterilization of water
for extraction of gold
for manufacture of bleaching powder
in synthesis of organic compounds like chloroform
in preparation of solvents like carbon tetrachloride
first poison gas released in war
identical the element
but suffused with both good and evil

Rocks

masses of consolidated minerals
of one or more types
hugging the global rim
most profuse being quartz
micas and feldspars
from mode of formation
three principal groups

sedimentary rocks
most numerous and of predominant import
deposits on land and sea
stratum by stratum
sequel of weathering and erosion
one group comprising elastic rocks
sprung from disintegration of other masses
and recumbent at bottom of seas and lakes
like shale and breccia
another born of chemical precipitation
mineral matter swimming in water
on evaporation left stranded
examples limestone and gypsum
a third memorials of organisms
like guano and coal

igneous rocks
molten in original state of magma
raging from below to crust of earth
settling into bosses sills dykes and necks
composition principally silicates
of lime magnesia alumina soda and potash
classification according to proportion of silica
the acid with highest amount
like granite and rhyolite
the intermediate with lesser quantity
like diorite and andesite
the basic with least
like serpentine and gabbro

Tan Kheng Yeang

metamorphic rocks
originally either of the other two
altered in construction and composition
by heat or pressure
often structure schistose
examples slate
a fine-grained rock
transformed by immense pressure
from sediments and volcanic matter
quartzite changed from quartz sandstone
into granular compact mass
gneiss a schistose material
of quartz mica and orthoclase
frequently come from granite

strange the forces and transformations
manipulating earths crust
formidably protracted the process
in terms of human time
but inexorable and ruthless
not to be expected that
whatever progress science may make
this ever will be stemmed
puissant the rocks
and perennial to us the mountains
but in their essence mutability

Fossils

relics of organisms
vegetable or animal
entrenched in crust of earth
and sleeping through aeons of antiquity
rarely complete animals
like mammoths embedded in ice
sometimes insects locked in amber
maybe only casts in clay or sand
or impressions in receptive material
or reproductions of organic structure
by molecular replacement
with mineral matter

fossilization dependent
on likelihood of outwitting decay
by enclosure in some suitable deposit
such rare on land
hence marine fossils preponderant
organisms with stubborn parts
more capable of bequeathing vestiges
more disturbed by earth movements
fossils in older formations
more fragmentary than in recent
preservation of but few living things
geological record deficient
revealing innumerable gaps

fossils of one layer
remains of sedimentary rock
of one particular period
gradual change of organisms
from age to age
fossils of successive strata
testimony to evolution

clues to geographic and climatic conditions
of epochs in the remote past
divulging existence of vanished lands seas and lakes
and drastic changes of climate
from fossils geological record determined
the stratified rocks classified and named
and relevant periods of time assigned

terrifying the lengthy succession
of living things that have vanished
history of life in zoic rocks
stupendous incredible
strange the durability of matter
in certain forms and circumstances
grand the spectacle of life
or sorry the tale
to each his reaction

Photosynthesis

formation of carbohydrates
the participants carbon dioxide
imbibed from air through stomata
and water from soil through roots
by athletic leaves of plants
the green chlorophyll
nestling in the minute protoplasmic chloroplasts
lapping up solar illumination
of which absence clasps etiolation

molecules of the gas and liquid
moulded by chemical magic in the chloroplasts
the sunlight drunk furnishing the energy
this the one process whereby
carbon dioxide resumes organic garb
and gleams the primary source of food

set free like captive bird
vital oxygen back to atmosphere
replacing that ruined
in respiration of living units
photosynthesis comatose
in hours of darkness
though no cessation of breathing
but its activity more intense
hence more diffusion into surroundings
of oxygen than carbon dioxide

simple plant nutrition
disdainful of complex organic food
instead from inorganic substances
organic sugar and starch
innocent form of nutrition
unlike animal slaying animal
a beneficial process
incidentally shooting out the element
essential to all life

Energy

an abstract phenomenon
the capacity to perform work
to move objects against resisting forces
like gravity and friction
to transform vehicles into racing entities
and endow machinery with life

many the shapes of energy
mechanical energy potential as in clock weights
and kinetic as in flying bullets
chemical energy as in petrol
electrical as in motors and generators
heat as in fire and steam
radiant as in light
nuclear as in the splitting of atoms

protean under certain conditions
in corresponding amounts
conservation of energy
not leaping from nothingness
or diving out of existence
original source of energy the sun
final link of chain

generation of heat
on eventual transformation of all energy
into heat at same temperature
cessation of life and activity

Clay

sedimentary rock material
sprung from weathering of land
principal constituent of clay
secondary flaky material
from chemical decomposition
of micas and feldspars
happily swung along by rivers
and relinquished in seas and estuaries
complex mineral content
main minerals aluminium silicates
other substances like
iron carbonates and sulphides
structure solid matter
with water strangled between the particles

of pronounced fineness in grain
colloidal in nature
with low internal friction
plastic cohesive and tenacious
smooth greasy and sticky
subject to shrinkage on drying
amount tied to plasticity
mouldable when wet
friable dry
impervious to water
inadvisable for foundations
of house to repose on bed
which contracts and expands
with variable liquid content
generating uneven settlement

kaolin pure white clay
from disintegration of granite
material for glamorous porcelain
brick clay sandy impure
from later rock formations
normally extracted from open pits
manufactured into ordinary bricks
fireclay fairly hard rook
plentiful below coal seams
almost bereft of lime iron and alkalis
invulnerable to intense heat
gifted for taking glaze
magnificent for firebricks and tiles

clay a substance common
unattractive unclean
become mud when drowned in water
yet serviceable for human purposes
in everything some worth

Limestone

stone of aggressive occurrence
bred in most geological systems
widely distributed throughout the globe
straddling extensive plains
or rearing into mountain ranges
a sedimentary rock
laid over lengthy periods of time
either chemically generated
or more commonly of organic origin
consisting of marine accumulations
of fossil shells and bones

manifest in several types
and beds of diverse thicknesses
from white to black in hue
readily subject to action of water
principal constituent calcium carbonate
with great range of purity
amount of clay even up to a third
silica in grain or colloidal form
varying in texture
from crystalline to dull and compact
tough and of low porosity
capable of carving with ease

travertine of pale tint
constituted of water solution deposits
fairly hard and compact
admirable haven for fossils
oolite like roe of fish
tiny spheres cemented into solid mass
chemical precipitates from seawater
mainly from mesozoic times
chalk of glorious purity
the whiter the purer
extremely soft and easily crumbling
marble recrystallized limestone
fruit of heat and pressure
granular in appearance
capable of taking high polish
of diverse colours
according to nature of other substances
dolomite double carbonate of magnesium and calcium
white or pinkish mineral
crystalline rhombohedral
liable to disintegrate on exposure

manifold the uses
as masonry in buildings
for carving into monuments
as metal in paving of roads
for manufacture of cement
for burning into lime
as flux for iron smelting
as aggregate for concrete
as filler in bitumen
for fertilization of plants
rock of magnificent service

Asbestos

fibrous silky mineral
located where magnesia prospers
an amphibole or a serpentine
commercially of greatest moment
chrysotile running as narrow veins
helter skelter through serpentine rock
heroic against fire
reluctant conductor of heat and electricity
antagonistic to fusion
disdainful of decay
spurning chemical change
happy to separate
into thin flexible strands
various its uses
for weaving into fireproof fabric
for lagging of steam pipes
for incombustible paints and paper
for fraternizing with portland cement
to issue as building material
by way of sheets and tiles
for cylinder packings and brake linings
as insulation for sound and electric cables
reduced to dust for filler in asphalt
peculiar mineral with unique properties

Division Four

Circling of Island

Here squats the ferry terminal where the impatient launches rest momentarily before galloping off to the mainland, a brief journey to Butterworth opposite. Vehicles slide in and out of the lanes sentinelled by ticket-selling booths—motorcars, lorries, motorcycles, bicycles. Pedestrians vanish through a side entrance and hurry to the upper decks of the launches by a segregated way. The car park is flabbergasted with exanimate vehicles. The road sweats with serried cars perforce awaiting their turn to crawl to the pier.

Rolling along Weld Quay and up Light Street past public offices and buildings and on to Farquhar Street past hotels, the car soon hies along Northam Road and Kelawei Road with their mansions in commodious compounds. Traffic is not demented at this hour of the morning, and the dishevelled trees on the roadside provide broad shade from the sun's luxuriant rays. But an impetuous car jumps out of a side road and rushes into the rear flank of a confidently careering vehicle; both yell to an agonized cessation and the drivers are standing on the road in fiery oratory over their cases!

Traffic growls the artificial incubus of the modern world. Our ancestors in the jungles were not tossed to death by mechanical monsters more sanguinary than tigers and wolves. It's singular that progress oft procreates its own retribution and science, which can unroll new forces, not rarely is unable to foresee and frustrate their effluvial effects. Accidents, lacerating or fatal, are so prevalent that mankind has shed its horror and grown well-nigh indifferent.

Scan the large circus at the junction of Kelawei Road and Bagan Jermal Road with its flowering plants. Royal palms at the periphery with their straight trunks stand sentries guarding the decorative fountain splashing at the centre. Fountains are never amiss; they lend an ineffable grace to any prospect or place with their diaphanous bliss.

Leaving behind the city's heterogeneous scene I whirl along Tanjong Tokong Road, skirting the sea. No paucity is discernible of restaurants splashing seafood—crabs and prawns and fish. This should be where the countryside strews its natural gems but bungalows and housing estates breathe jauntily all along the road. Is this a manifestation of progress of the population explosion or desecration of nature?

Heaves into view the village of Tanjong Bungah, just a row of shop-houses on one side and another of restaurants adjoining the beach. Nothing entrancing wraps the habitations; without them this little cape would distil more glamour. The purity of the beach teeming with living shells and lapped by green waves, the coconut palms with their feathers afloat, the gambolling breezes—these still have being but in attenuated form.

Now the road serpentines along the hillside. Below a translucent, picturesque beach dispersed rocks sit on the brown sands in amorphous dignity. The green sea lies peaceful, shimmering beneath the vociferous sun. Swimmers recline a few steps from the water's edge bliss-enwrapped. Out at sea, boats paddle lazily along. Scattered bungalows for holiday makers nestling close to the shore flash past. To vitiate this glamorous stretch of beach by commercial development is philistinism at its nadir, but already in the name of tourism big hotels have commenced to effuse their cold warmth.

Tourism—should it be dressed in encomiastic garb? Every country becomes an interior decorator to attract foreign exchange in this facile way. It is a parasitic trade, unproductive, and the direct beneficiaries are tour operators, hotel keepers, transport workers, and tradesmen. The tourist is lured to see natural scenes that leave him unimpressed and historical relics that are to him just ruins. Other people's sacred customs are recreational curiosities. Does he appreciate cultural glories? Still, tourism is salutary for crushing the exclusivism of nations and inducing them to feel they belong to one race, humankind.

Batu Ferringhi spreads a straggling place, looking out on a scintillating bay flanked by a couple of miles of golden sand, most beautiful of beaches. Serenity roams the locality; crowds obtrude not their raucous presence. Attap huts nestle amid their coconut plantations on the other side of the road. With the blue sky above, this rural scene looks idyllic.

On glides the car westward along a smooth, level length of coastal road. One can gaze far out into the ocean with the sun shimmering on it. Soon comes Telok Bahang, a fishing village. Trawlers are visible in the distance, and nearer the fishermen are busy catching with small nets. A life of toil and peril—would Isaak Walton relish it?

The journey has been shooting westwards all this while. Now it swerves south and the scenery changes. The sea though at no considerable distance is imperceptible and the road wigwags its discomfort. But another village and the road resumes its level character.

Plantations of diverse sorts roll into view. See the slender but stalwart rubber trees and the coconut palms, some hovering at a perilous angle. They are not in season now, but soon those trees will be fructuous with durians and those mangosteens and those rambutans. A delightful spectacle is the banana plants with their broad leaves and in plenitude of production the whole year weaves.

Balik Pulau, on the opposite side of the island to the city, is where prances in pride the nutmeg industry. There go the lumbering lorries conveying the raw produce from the estates to the factories. Oil for curative purposes is extracted from the seeds. The renitent flesh is sliced in diverse patterns, sweetened, and packed wet in plastic bags. It may be reduced to shreds and dried under the sun's rapacious rays.

The road plunges once more into rugged sinuosity. Dark, tree-clad hills exude a clammy feel; the savage sun is forced to fume in frustration. Light moulds the mind with weight; bright scenes lift and the dark oppress.

Past Telok Kumbar on the southern coast I come to Bayan Lepas, where squats an airfield. A plane has just kicked off the ground and is flying towards Singapore; it grows fainter and soon has disappeared among the clouds. Not so many years ago, aircraft swooped a sensation and a hazard; they have grown commonplace and are no less imbued with safety than railway trains. Progress nowadays gallops at a rapid pace, and an invention develops with stirring sequel in phenomenally brief time.

From this place the road sings in level smoothness and laughs its way through open country. But factory areas and housing estates have commenced to stare at the route from either side; fields suffer attenuation, and what will thrive will not be a rural landscape but a linear town. This category of development makes the locality neither a town nor the countryside; it is an undiluted evil spoiling nature unto no purpose. A town should be a compact area with definite boundaries; straggling suburbs are struggling monstrosities.

There stands the small, century-old Snake Temple beloved of tourists. As temples go, it is an unimpressive affair, but it is enwreathed with a distinguished feature. Curled round incense burners and lying on altars are numerous small, green snakes, poisonous vipers, but lulled in this smoky atmosphere into somnolent, inoffensive creatures. Professional photographers plan pictures of tourists thrilled to acquire mementos of themselves dangling live serpents. Thus, a place of worship has become an exhibition booth and sightseers are more conspicuous than votaries.

Now approaches Glugor, where bloom a university, a teachers' training college, and an aquarium in pleasant environs. Cultural amenities never glow less appealing, and any effort to provide the best is never too expensive. Though culture is good per se, it does not shine so to the ordinary man; to be palatable it has to forge a nexus with amusement or livelihood. This does not scale the peak of idealism, but it is on higher land than the swamp of no culture, than the jungle of pleasure and occupation hanging on graceless militarism or gross materialism.

Onward sweeps the car to Bukit Dumbar Park, an area of fair extent housing an underground reservoir beneath a flat hillock. The ground heaves huge sighs of unevenness, and no beautiful pavilions or picturesque pools sit smiling. A single motor-road climbs from the entrance. But flowers glow in varied profusion, playing with the tireless breeze. A park is an artificial entity, an attempt to reproduce nature. The best park is one least moulded by the hand of man.

Jelutong, an unsavoury place that development has left behind, could be annihilated without any loss and transformed into a tidy town. Whether a hamlet crouches far away from a civic area or near it or is accounted within its legal confines is no reason for relegating it to a squalid existence. Any community should enjoy pleasant surroundings. The scene here is neither rural nor urban but commingles the worst of both. Dinginess is the manifest lamina; there breathes not the fresh beauty of natural landscapes or the purposive elegance of human works. The most visible evidence of civilization is the way the environment of a community is moulded to stay.

Back within the city area and rolling along roads with depressing factories and godowns and over silted unsightly rivers, I emerge on to Weld Quay and come to where I started. This journey of forty-odd miles round the perimeter of Penang Island would not easily elude memory's spider clasp.

The Tragedy of Life

Life is one protracted tragedy, its sorrows multitudinous, multifarious. The innumerable forms wriggled out in the course of slow scowling evolution, Homo sapiens the terminal rung in the creaking ladder.

The process is a horrifying groan, a long-drawn ordeal. It is ineffably strange, this evolution, this torment sliding along an unbroken string of aeons. Creature slew and devoured creature; whole species were catapulted into nothingness by environment. What is the purport of such life? The organic entities arose and vanished through the law of necessity; they did not choose; left to them, would they have willed to leap into being?

Primitive man writhed a terrible life. Joylessly, he squirmed in his cave at night. When day scattered its light he was engrossed in one thing, the procurement of food; he stalked his prey, assassination gleaming in his eye; in turn he might fall the booty of wild beasts. Man fought man venomously to slaughter, even to consume. Later some implements were invented and some discoveries plaited; dwellings were erected and fields cultivated. But filthy were the abodes and what toil wrapped agriculture. Weapons were evolved for more efficient extermination. People congregated in tribes, and mass massacres gloated and grovelled.

In civilization hobbled and the arts panted and knowledge glinted. But did joy encircle life? The masses tottered under incessant toil in misery's unbreakable coil. Towns grew haphazard where prowled robbers and murderers. Autocratic systems of political organization induced intoxicated inhumanity; civil and foreign wars engendered gruesome holocausts. In modern times strut an exuberant array of conveniences and pleasures. Life may hover above the grisly pit it stood in before, but sorrow surpasses happiness still; the streets lie death-traps; all species of disasters, natural and artificial, still roam.

Nature evinces indifference to human welfare. Earthquakes ever and anon prance in this part of the world or that; their brothers, the volcanoes, roar and belch forth their fiery forces. Rocks come crashing down wantonly in landslides. Floods stampede out of the rivers to ravage their enemy, the land. Hurricanes trumpet their might, lightning kills, and rain drowns. Drought slaps fertile fields into wasteland.

Countless ills lie in wait to invade the body. Any part, any organ, can sustain damage that begets pain in greater or lesser degree. Of the materials sustaining life air abounds, water may sometimes spring havoc, while food has to be won with toil, and myriads suffer or perish of hunger. Bacteria make battle and wreak destructive woe. Strange the numerous varieties of invisible adversaries lurking in all corners! The human organism is a frail entity, a creaky machine, a miserable contrivance, a product of aeons of uneasy, unsystematic evolution.

The pains evolved by man himself are no less grievous. His emotions are mostly productive of misery. Hate, jealousy, anger, despair, revengefulness, remorse, malice, yearning, and fear are fraught with distress.

Joys terminate in satiety. Ignorance grows branches of woes. Suffering and death ensue from misapprehension of the causes of diseases and inability to treat them. People may do things or lead ways of life entailing disastrous consequences.

Superstitions weave a web of misery. Religions preach tragic mendacity; the fanciful figures of deities and demons and the baleful beliefs produce more fatuous fear than rhythmic reality. Philosophy unknots no problems but only breeds bewildered obfuscation. Science aspires to make life easier, but it has its limitations, and lethal inventions scatter pain and death. Art creates mental realms of wan illusory bliss or saddening if moulded after reality.

Humans have formed society and failed to live in harmony. They endeavour to exploit, maltreat, or dominate one another; gossips breathe scandal, merchants cheat, politicians bluff, the strong oppress the weak. Thieves and robbers grasp what is not theirs; thugs murder. Psychopaths wreak their dangerous urges.

The state, organization of force and fear, has ground out more evil than good. It has only served to sanction robbery and oppression. From it springs that apogee of madness, war, with its monstrous suffering, its massacres en masse, its filth, its barbaric cruelty, its senselessness, its reprisals and counter-reprisals, its espionage, its treachery, its evocation of atavistic instincts. It is in war that the tragedy of life clutches its climax. Always it has discharged its fevered yell, but with novel inventions grows more fell.

Ferine roar the varied assemblage of afflictions. But those forged by man are more disastrous; if these were tossed out, the world would be much less sorrow-soaked. It is a weird crime, a ludicrous folly, for man to augment his stinging load when all his efforts should be focused on natural traumas. His rough environment does not smile benign; he is not born dowered with joy. It is for him to fashion a happy world; thus animus of man against man is inexcusable. Unclouded bliss will never be his breath; the race of misery ends with agonized death. But his brief life he can mould to less tragic shape.

The Parking Attendant

AA slides out of school and can't get a job. He hunts here and there, weaves scores of applications, and answers any advertisement hitting his way. Prospective employers, a superior breed, sometimes deign to note and wave him to an interview. Questions and observations—some facetious, some fantastic, mostly familiar—are hurled; success, though, never seeps into his world.

With clipped wings he hobbles into the ranks of parking attendants. Paid a pittance he eludes starvation, but he accounts the work senseless and smothering. A car sidles into a parking bay; he saunters towards it and indites a notice that chants the time and car number; he displays it on the windshield behind a wiper. In course of time he is hailed by the driver and, on receiving the requisite rent, replies with a receipt.

He never envisaged while in school he would be trammelled in this empty employment. He was dedicated to introspection, to daydreaming; he had spun ambitious plans of performing exalted work; he was not cast in ordinary mould. But lacking practicality, he did not really know what to do, how to set about bringing his aspirations to fruition. He yearned to help the world, but aid was his desideratum and nobody cared to sprinkle it on him.

BB gravitates to the same street, likewise a parking attendant. She is pretty and vivacious. He catapults into love but with its helm revolving only in fantasy's realm. He dares not avouch it lest rejection and ridicule torment him; he holds it finer to cherish his sentiments like treasured arcane.

Rolls in a company director in a scintillating vehicle. His wife has died recently. His gaze brushes BB and his heart pumps towards her; soon they are going out together. AA observes in paralyzed helplessness. What could he do? Later shoots the news; BB is married. He mopes; he does not fume. He cannot unglue her from his mind.

Disgust with his job and he hurls it off. He performs odd tasks; he is fleetly flagellated by society to the condition of a tramp. He can never hug the ways of the world; he does not think as his fellows do; he'll never catch normal success.

He rambles to the seashore. He sits on a rock and broods over the waves; they rush against his seat and the spray wets him. He sinks into a dream of BB, and his countenance radiates rapturous gleam. Shifting to his present hapless state he suffers agony. His mind is cloaked in slumberousness. A storm arises and he falls into the billows and drowns.

About the Author

Born around the time of the foundation of the Republic of China, in the former English colony of British Malaya, Tan Kheng Yeang was educated in an English school. His father was from China but had emigrated to Malaya and had become a successful businessman, involved in various activities, including as a rubber merchant. From his early days the author was interested in literature and philosophy and as his interest evolved to science, he decided to study civil engineering at the University of Hong Kong, as he felt he needed a practical career.

After the Japanese occupied Hong Kong, he fled into free China where he found work in an office constructing roads and later an airfield in Guangxi Province. After the war ended in 1945, he returned to Malaya and became an engineer in the City Council of Georgetown, Penang. After his retirement, he worked as an engineering consultant. He is the author of twelve books that reflect the broad range of his interests and talents.